Creative Discipline

Tyona Benton

Dedication

I dedicate this book to my mom who instilled in me that I can do anything I put my mind to. To my husband who is supportive and has been compassionate, understanding on this new journey. To my son, Frederick and daughter, Falana, two amazing children. To Ms Dee who challenged me to complete this book.

About the Author

I am a wife, mother of two, and Certified Parenting Instructor. A native to Los Angeles, California. I come from a family of community advocates. I have worked with children for over 20 years through babysitting, volunteering at schools, volunteering in kids' corners, after-school programs, and more.

I love kids and watching their minds develop. I enjoy helping children of all ages. I choose to think outside of the box to engage children in exploring and pushing them to stretch outside of their comfort zone. I believe that children need and desire discipline. I choose to use discipline as a way to increase children's writing, listening, and understanding.

Table of Contents

My Start with Creative Discipline

When I was 19 years old, I took a parenting class. I didn't have children at the time. However, I volunteered at my little cousin's school, and they offered the parenting class for free. I learned so much during those 10 weeks. Two of the main things I learned that the disciplinary action should fit the offence and timeout has just as much to do with the parent cooling down as it does with the child.

Consistency is the key to good discipline. If you tell your child that you are going to take something away the next time, you must follow through with what you said. Making a hollow threat is only bad news for you, the parent because your child knows that you won't follow through. When keeping your word during discipline, you are teaching your child that you will keep your commitment and that they should always keep their word.

Over the years I developed creative ways to discipline the children around me and my own. In this book, you will find my top four methods. Not every action does require a big reaction. When your child does something that you don't like, a pet peeve, talking about it and giving future consequences can surely stop the behavior.

By talking to your child, you give them words, so they can express themselves. Allowing your child to use words instead of tantrums makes parenting easier. When you speak out problems with your child introduce vocabulary words. This will enhance the conversations and increase your child's understanding.

Talk about It

When I was a kid, and I did something that I had no business doing my mom would punish me with a long talk. She would explain how disappointed she was with my actions. Then she would tell me an extremely long story with tons of details about her childhood, what I called her war stories. The worst part was I had to sit still and just listen. Then she would make sure I was listening by asking me questions like "what do you think happened?" or "you know what your grandmother did to me?" The war story would go on and on. Inside I wished I would have made a better decision.

Little people between the ages 2-4 have short attention spans. When talking with them about their actions, it is best to make it short and straightforward. I found that if you have the child touch your nose with their finger, they will focus on you. If you find that their eyes or head are still wondering around the room, then ask for both hands to touch your nose. Then in a gentle tone explain what was done incorrectly and state your expectations. Give a hug and move on.

For ages 5-7 even though their attention span has grown, it is still not very long. You can tell your child one of your short war stories or a scenario that is similar to their action. Explain how the decision that you made and what you would change if you could go back in time. Ask them if they understand, then have them explain what they understand. Give a hug and move on. If you see your child is about to make, the same mistake offer a reminder.

Children 8 and up can handle a complete war story with all the details. Have them sit down with you as you share a moment of your history with them. Ask questions to make sure they are following you. If your child seemed to zone out, then rewind your story. You will get to share your past with them. They will think about making a bad decision the next time because war stories go on forever. Once you have finished your point ask, "Do you understand why that was a bad decision?" and "What did you get out of the story I just shared with you?" Give a hug and move on.

If your child does something that you don't approve of and your past does not give you an example tell about one of your friends or something you saw on T.V. I use this method with my son. Sometimes he does things that neither my husband nor I would do. When that happens, I talk about different ways the situation could have turned out. I ask him to take himself out of the equation and what advice would he give. Ending these moments with a hug allows your child to know that you still love them even though they made a mistake. Moving on from that moment helps us, the parents, keep our sanity.

Expressing Emotion

Have you ever been so emotional that you can't formulate the words to express how you feel? Then you just scream. I have, and so have more children. I remember when my son was a toddler and he would get upset although he tried to tell me how he felt I couldn't always understand. He would become frustrated and just scream. I wanted to scream too because I didn't understand why he was frustrated. Then I realized he was emotional and needed to verbalize his emotion.

Verbalize Emotion

My definition of verbalize emotion is putting words to feelings in a clam tone and sometimes even examples. The question may come to mind: if I am upset how can I be clam? The answer is simple to remove yourself from the situation. You have the right to take a moment and calm down. Take a deep breath and release the frustration (make a noise like a flat tire while releasing your breath) and clear your mind. Now you are able to verbalize your emotion. Translating your feelings into words allows you to understand your own feelings, find the root of the issue, and communicate with others what triggered you to react the way you did.

Crying

Sometimes we are taught that crying is a sign of weakness. The truth is crying helps get rid of the chemicals that the stress produced in your body. Crying helps reduce pain. When we choose to hold in the negative feelings, we only hurt our self. If you see your child wanting to release feelings through tears, let them know you are here for them and check in periodically. Be available when your child is ready to talk, remember to listen, and acknowledge their feelings. If your child seems to linger in this crying state, ask what can we (child and parent) do to make this better or what choices could have been made to make it, so you are not in this position again?

Talking about Emotions

When talking about emotions, you cannot be judgmental. Remember that emotions are personal and are not always logical. A good rule of thumb is to verbalize and acknowledge the emotions then break down the feelings. Breaking down the feelings means no one is at fault because we are dealing with the emotions and calming down. After emotions have been released then talk about decision-making skills, consequences (if necessary), coping skills, and an emotional solution.

Here is an example.
Verbalize emotion: My feeling is hurt because Ally didn't share her toy.

Breaking down the emotion: Parent: Why are your feelings hurt because Ally didn't share her toy? Is it because Ally is your friend and you feel that she should share her toys with you? (Give your child the opportunity to answer the questions)

Acknowledging Emotion: I understand that Ally is your friend and she didn't share her toy.

Find an emotional solution: Did you express to Ally that she hurt your feelings because she didn't share her toy?

Write it Out

I remember as a teenager getting into a fight at a high school basketball game. A boy kept throwing paper at my friends and me. I walked over to him and asked him "Why are you throwing paper at us? Stop throwing paper at my friends and me." The boy jumped up, pushed me, and we started fighting. After everything was over, we were both suspended from school for a few days. My mom was so disappointed with me. She didn't want to talk about it. I couldn't believe that she didn't want to know what happened. She told me "when we get home, I want you to write out everything that happened before you got into the fight all the way to what happened after the fight." I was so upset; however, writing out what happened allowed me to see that I should have asked an adult to handle the situation.

Ages 3-5

For this age group writing out what happened is too advanced. Have them draw a picture about what happened, and then explain the picture as you write it down. Together read what happened. Then talk about their feelings and what techniques could have been used to make the situation better. Use this opportunity to help your child develop decision-making skills and impulse control. Ask your child leading question to give them the chance to find solutions.

Sample leading questions:
- Who do you think you could ask for help?
- What should you do next time?
- How could you have asked?
- Should we hit our friends?
- How did this make you feel?

Ages 6 & 7

These ages are learning to write and give some details about stories. Have them answer the who, what, when, where, and how. Then go over the answers allowing them to give more detail. This exercise helps your child improve their writing skills. As a parent, you can see where your child is. You may choose to give a leading question and open-ended questions.

Sample questions
- Who was involved?
- Who saw what happened?
- Who was the adult in authority?
- Where was the adult?
- What were you doing just before the incident occurred?
- What was the outcome?
- How will you handle this situation should it happen again?

Ages 8 and up

By this age children can write stories, book reports, and give lots of details.

Give these instructions:
- Write in complete sentences.

- Write the who, what, where, when, why, and how in essay form.
- Include the names of other individuals that witnessed the event.
- Write what choices you could made to make it a better situation.
- Give a due time (should be the same day of the incident)

Extra:

- Ask what disciplinary action should be taken
- Rewrite the essay with all necessary corrections

The purpose of this exercise is to improve writing skills, handle timed writing, and become more detailed. When you receive the essay of what happened read it then go over it with your child. Ask questions, check grammar, and punctuation.

Writing out what happened is a disciplinary action and a learning tool. Using this method will help your child in school and to make better life choices.

Research

My son runs off frequently. Something interesting catches his eye, and off he goes. Over the years he has gotten better, however, it has not stopped, and now my daughter is running off after. My son has been running off since he was two years old. I used to become very frantic and sometimes would even cry. Then I learned to stay in the same place and yell his name. However, the other day my daughter ran off. This is not her normal behavior. Then I realized that she ran off because she sees her brother do it. I explained to her how running off is not okay and that someone could take her. Then I told my son "You are one of your sister's leaders and you have led her wrong. When we get home, I would like you to research human trafficking. Then write at least 20 sentences about what you learned and present this to me." Was he happy about this no, however, he learned a lot.

This tool is best used with children 8 and up, however for younger children you may find some kid videos.

How do you use research as a discipline tool?
- Have your child look up their action, read an article or two and watch a few videos.
- Then give a verbal and written report. (If your child is younger a verbal report is sufficient.)
- Ask questions after the report is given to make sure the child understands.

This tool teaches your child how to find answers about things that they don't know. I think research is one of the best things you can do in life. You get to understand how things work, what is the best, the worst, past and present. I love the knowledge that I gain while researching.

The Fish Bowl Game

Some years back my aunt was talking to me about her youngest daughter. She explained that she would turn twelve soon and her attitude was changing. My aunt was at her wit's end with her daughter smacking her teeth and head rocking from side to side when she talked to her. It was that day that I came up with the Fish Bowl Game. My aunt went home that night and wrote all of her daughter's birthday presents on small pieces of paper and put them in a jar. She called her daughter in and explained when you choose to be disrespectful, do not complete your choirs, or smack your teeth you will pull from this jar. Inside the jar are all of your birthday presents, as you pull items you will not get those things for your birthday. Within a few days, her daughter got a pass and lost a birthday present. When she lost the birthday present, she realized that being disrespectful and not following directions was not the way she wanted to go.

Ages 6-12

You can take away things that they were going to get (like a birthday present) or things that they love to use or play with (i.e. internet usage, favorite toy, sports, extra classes, etc.). When taking away things that the child likes to play with or use, a time frame must be given.

Ages 12-17

You can take away gifts for upcoming holidays, future weekends, electronics, allowance, etc. Teenagers love to hang out so taking away the next weekend will make them feel like it's okay until they make plans for the upcoming weekend and can't go. When it comes to electronics, give a time when the child needs to turn in the electronic (internet, cell phone, TV, etc.,). If you give your child an allowance, you could have them pay you all or a portion.

I love the Fish Bowl Game because I don't get upset when my child doesn't follow directions, I didn't have to create a discipline action my child gets to pull the discipline action, and it changes with the different things that he likes. He may pull a "Pass" or lose something. Either way, I get to keep my cool.

What you will need:
- Paper
- Container (bowl, bag, container, hat, etc.)
- Pen

1. Cut the paper into small pieces (large enough to write on)
2. Write what you are taking away from the child
3. Write "Pass" on 3-5 of the pieces
4. Fold all the pieces of paper into small squares
5. Place into the container
6. When the child chooses not to follow directions, is disrespectful, etc. draw a line

through, write the date, and place the item lost on a place that the child frequently passes (i.e. refrigerator)

7. If your child needs to be reminded about the negative behavior, simply write the reason why the item was lost under the date.